Y0-ACM-111

You've Got Social Manners!

Party Pointers from A to Z
for Kids of All Ages

by Louise Elerding

You've Got Social Manners!
Party Pointers from A to Z
for Kids of All Ages

Written and Illustrated by Louise Elerding
Layout and Color Design by Bruce Gordon

Copyright ©2005 Louise Elerding
All Rights Reserved
including the right of reproduction in whole or in part in any form.

Grandy Publications
Burbank, California

ISBN 13: 978-0-9729237-4-3
ISBN 10: 0-9729237-4-8
Library of Congress Control Number: 2005931790

Other books written by Louise Elerding:
You've Got Manners! Table Tips from A to Z for Kids of All Ages
You've Got Manners! (portable handbook)
Ya tienes buenos modales! Consejitos de A a Z Para niños de todas edades
The Art of Expression Through Fashion Feng Shui
Formulas For Dressing The Whole Person

To order additional books, call 800-326-8953 or email MannersA2Z@aol.com
Visit us at www.youvegotmanners.com

Printed in China

Dedication

To Alyson and Kristin, my two precious daughters, who were adorable children and today are remarkable parents. Their natural awareness and modeling of sound values and good social skills to their five children is my inspiration for these books.

Acknowledgments
(In A to Z Order)

Advisory Board: Alyssa, Amanda, Emily, Jason, and Tyler — the five joys that make my heart sing, and always have such smart ideas!

Annette "KEED" Milionis — a treasured friend and utterly loyal supporter ever since we met and became best buddies in the 9th grade.

Cheerleaders with extraordinary support and innermost personal connection: Angie Michael, Bev McCord, Bonnie Hoskins, Brenda Kinsel, Cindy Miller, Evana Maggiore, Jacquie Pergola, Joyce Moore, Karenlee Mannerino, Lani Ridley, Maggie Agler, Marj Anderson, Nancy Thompson, Nannette Holland, Olivia Collins, Pam Gefke, Renee Lefko, Roberta Holt, Susie Deweese, and Sylvie Sauve.

Michael Vezo — dubbed "Michael the Archangel" — for his stable advice, realistic perspectives, and supreme enthusiasm; without him, these books would not be.

Signa Elerding — my mannerly Mother-in-law who we dub the "Queen of Social Graces." She demonstrated, by example, how to host parties with style. And to the descending branches of her family tree, all my treasured family who continue to enlighten me.

PARTY POINTERS
from A to Z

par.ty *(par/tee), n.* **a social get-together for talking, food, and fun.**

point.ers *(poin-ters), n.* **a piece of advice, especially on how to succeed in a specific area.**

so.cial *(so/shel), adj.* **about friendly companionship**

Taking good manners with you to parties and places is always welcome.
People who are polite guests are nice to have around.

You will always be able to show good social manners if you just ask yourself this question:
"Is what I am doing considerate of the other people and circumstances around me?"

Come along through these pages and see how many of these social manners you have used.
With all of you working together as the Considerate Crew,
our world is going to be filled with well-mannered, awesome kids.

Hi!

We are Polly Politely and Milton Manners here to show you how easy it is to have good manners while having a great time at parties and fun places.

We've invited our cousins Alyssa Appropriate, Amanda Mannerly, and Tyler Tactful here to play with us while we learn ways of being polite guests.

Let's take a look at how you can be the "Social Star" that everyone wants to have around.

A

Always ask if it's OK before turning on the TV in someone else's home.
Be "power-button" polite.

Please come to my party at 3:00.

Arriving at parties on time — no more than 10 minutes past the invited time — makes you "party punctual."

Be super nice and write a thank-you note when you can. It can be on email – or on real paper! This tells people that you really appreciate what they did for you.

Before going in to breakfast, after you've spent the night at a friend's house, spiff up: wash your face, brush your teeth, and comb your hair.

Cleaning up after yourself when you are a guest in someone's house is helpful.
You can take your empty dishes to the sink, pick up your socks,
and put away games and toys.

Computers often call you to come play – but if it's not your computer, ask the owner if you may use it.

Dates and social plans that need to be cancelled should not wait until the last minute. If you are ill, or can't attend, you or your Mom call as soon as possible.

Doors that you hold open for other girls, boys, and adults, show grown-up manners.

Eye contact is important when you are meeting people.
No looking down at your shoes. Instead, heads up and look right into
the bright eyes of the person you are being introduced to!

Excusing yourself from the table when you are finished shows respect to your hostess. Say, "May I please be excused?"

Finish your "first" helping of food before asking if you can have "seconds."
Check to see if there is enough for others who would like some too.

Hey Emily – Meet Tyler. He just won the school spelling bee.

Hi there Jason, Remember Alyssa? She's the one who is tough to beat at "Kings In the Corner".

Hi Tyler ~ This is Amanda. She's the fastest runner on the team.

Hello Alyssa – This is Jason. He's the best when it comes to math and numbers.

Hiya Amanda, Here comes Emily. She always sings in our talent shows – and wins!

Say one nice thing about each person and that will help them have something to start talking about to each other.

Friends of yours who don't know each other will feel better when you introduce them.

Good sportsmanship while playing games keeps the party happy.
Be a good winner and a smiling loser.

Gifts like to land in the hands of the person they are meant for. Give the special gift directly to your friend, or your hostess. Say something nice as you hand them your present, like… "I thought of you when I saw this. I hope you like it."

Helping yourself to food from your friend's refrigerator and cupboards could be risky. If you're starving, ask nicely if there is something you may have.

Households have rules. When you are the visitor, fit in with whatever those rules are. Maybe there is a room that is off-limits to food, such as "no eating in the living room."

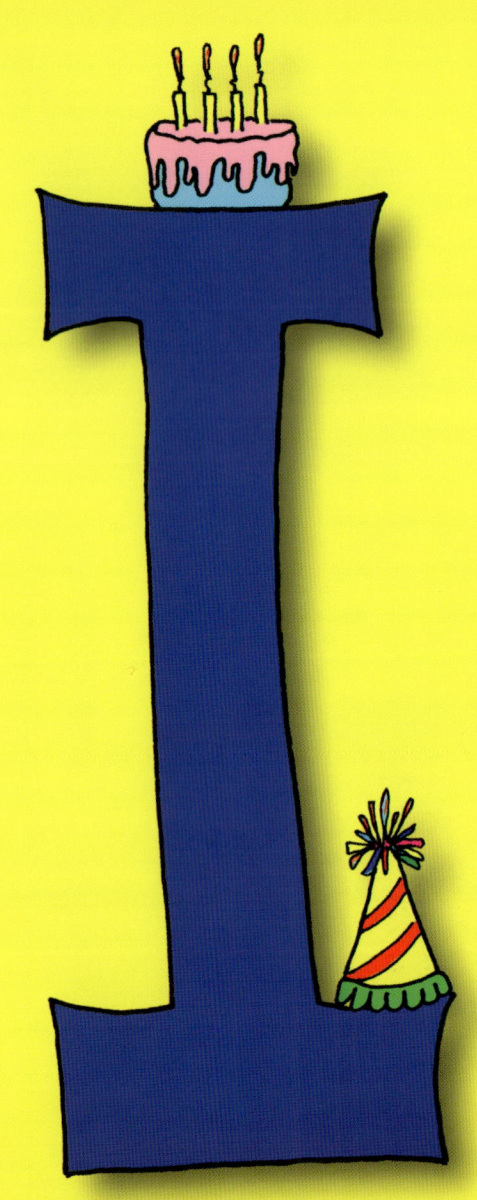

If it's a birthday party, make time to go over to the birthday-kid you are celebrating, and say a sincere "Happy Birthday + their name."

If you don't like the games, play anyway. Don't be a party-pouter.

Jokes make a party really fun. Be sure the story does not hurt someone's feelings on purpose.

Join in to help clean up after the party. Wipe up any spills you see on tables or carpets. Offer to put away leftover food, and help take out the trash.

Keep your word if you promise to do something for a friend. A promise is a promise!

Knock-knock ~ ? Knock before opening any closed door – like the bathroom, a bedroom, or an office.

Let your friends choose what they'd like to do when they are invited to your house. Take turns choosing what to play, and give everyone a chance to go first.

Listen instead of doing tons of talking. Listeners learn and make the best pals!

Maybe a very quiet person is really a shy person.
Make him feel a part of the group by asking him a question like
"Who is your teacher this year?" This could start a new friendship.

Make your bed or roll up your sleeping bag and pillow when you have been to a sleepover at a friend's house. Pack up all of your belongings when it's time to leave, and be on time when your ride comes to get you.

Not your fault...but, oops, you broke something. Tell the person it belongs to right away...and see what you can do to help fix or mend it.

Name yourself and the family who lives there, when you answer the phone in someone else's home. Say, "Hello, this is the Smith residence... Alyssa speaking." Then offer to take a message.

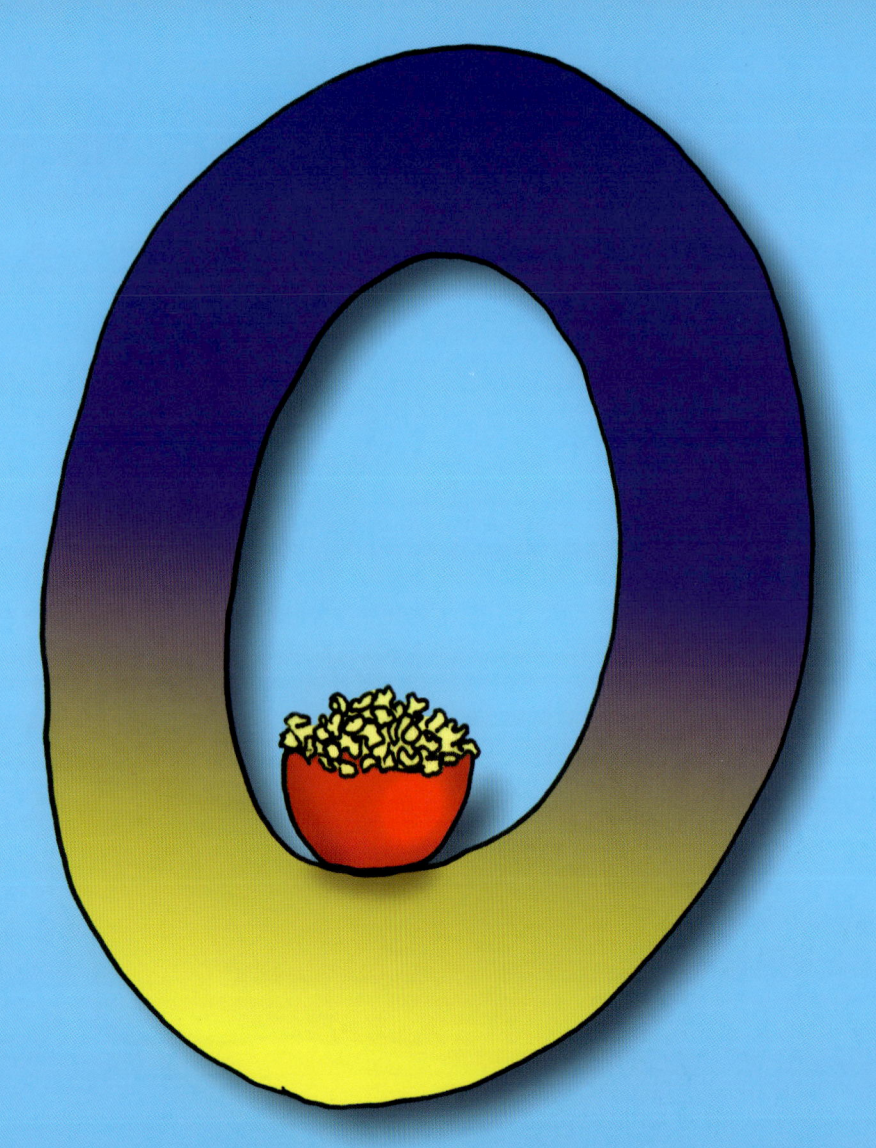

Offer a snack to your houseguests, and share whatever you are eating when munching & crunching in front of someone else.
Share other things too - like toys, books, & games.

Overnight gear needs to have a good place to land. Ask your hostess where she would like you to put your things; don't just drop them anywhere.

Playing with all of the friends you've invited over is important; do not ignore anyone that you asked to come and play with you. Be equally nice to everyone.

Place the toilet seat in the DOWN position before you leave the bathroom. Remember that's what it's made for. It's a cover, it's a lid, it's a round "door" that needs closing ... GOOD KID!

SH-SH-SH

Quiet voices and quiet activities are polite when you are up early and no one else in the house is awake yet.

Quickly stand up when someone new is being introduced to you, or is coming into the room to meet you. It makes them feel special.

R

RSVP means "please reply" in French. Always answer an invitation that is given to you, either "yes" or "no" – and do it as soon as you can.

Rearranging furniture in someone else's house isn't a great idea – unless you're getting paid as their furniture mover! Leave beds, lamps, and tables where they are.

Smile and say "goodbye" and "thank you for inviting me" to your friend and their parent when you are leaving their house or the party.

Shake hands and say something friendly when someone puts their hand out to shake yours.

Take time out to let another person finish talking before you interrupt them with what you want to say. Take turns talking and listening to each other.

To be the receiver of gifts is very fun. Be sure to say a smiley "thank-you," and add something nice about the present, like… "I'll have fun with this!"

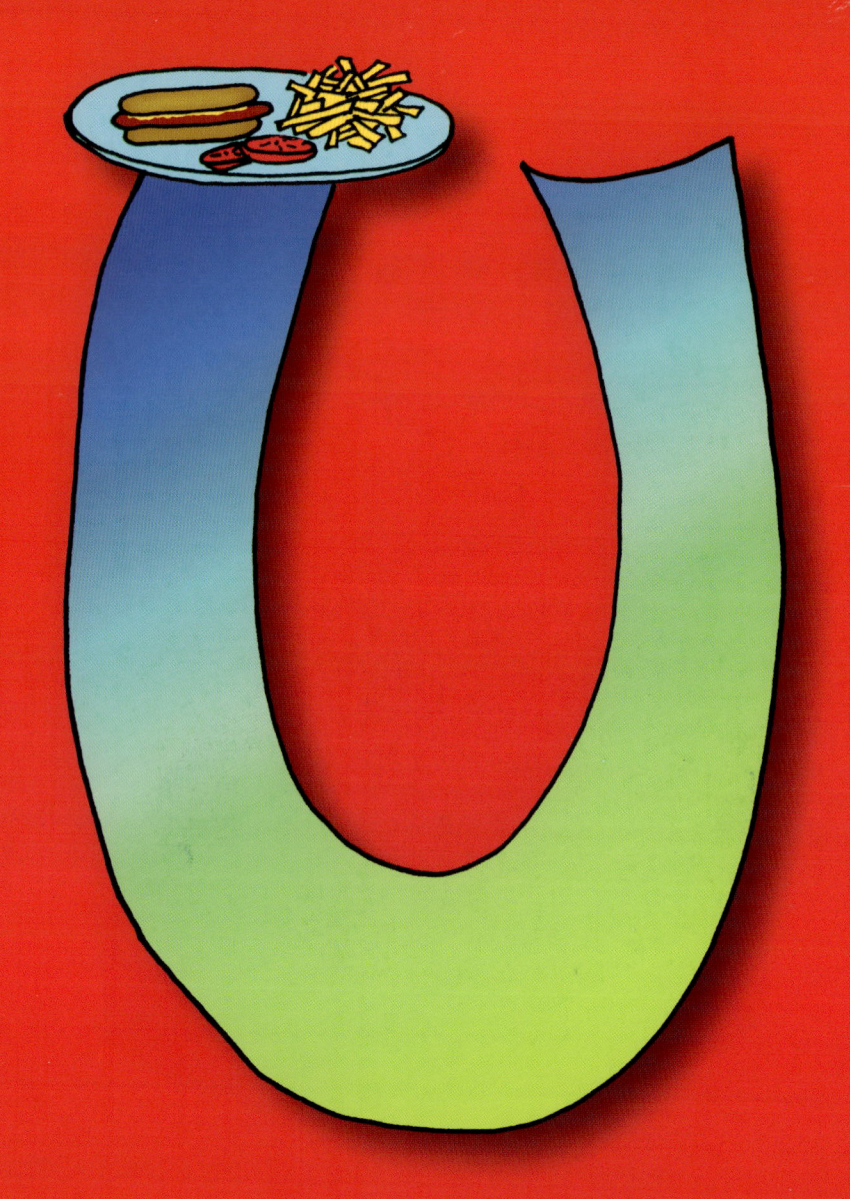

Unless you are offered a choice of foods at a mealtime, don't ask for something else that is not being served.

Using the phone in someone else's home needs permission. Asking first is always polite and appreciated.

Very good guests pay attention to when a party invitation has an "ending time." Plan to leave by the ending time stated.

Visiting elderly relatives will be nice if you bring them something to see — pictures of you in school activities, sports, or places you have been. You can also bring them something you have made.

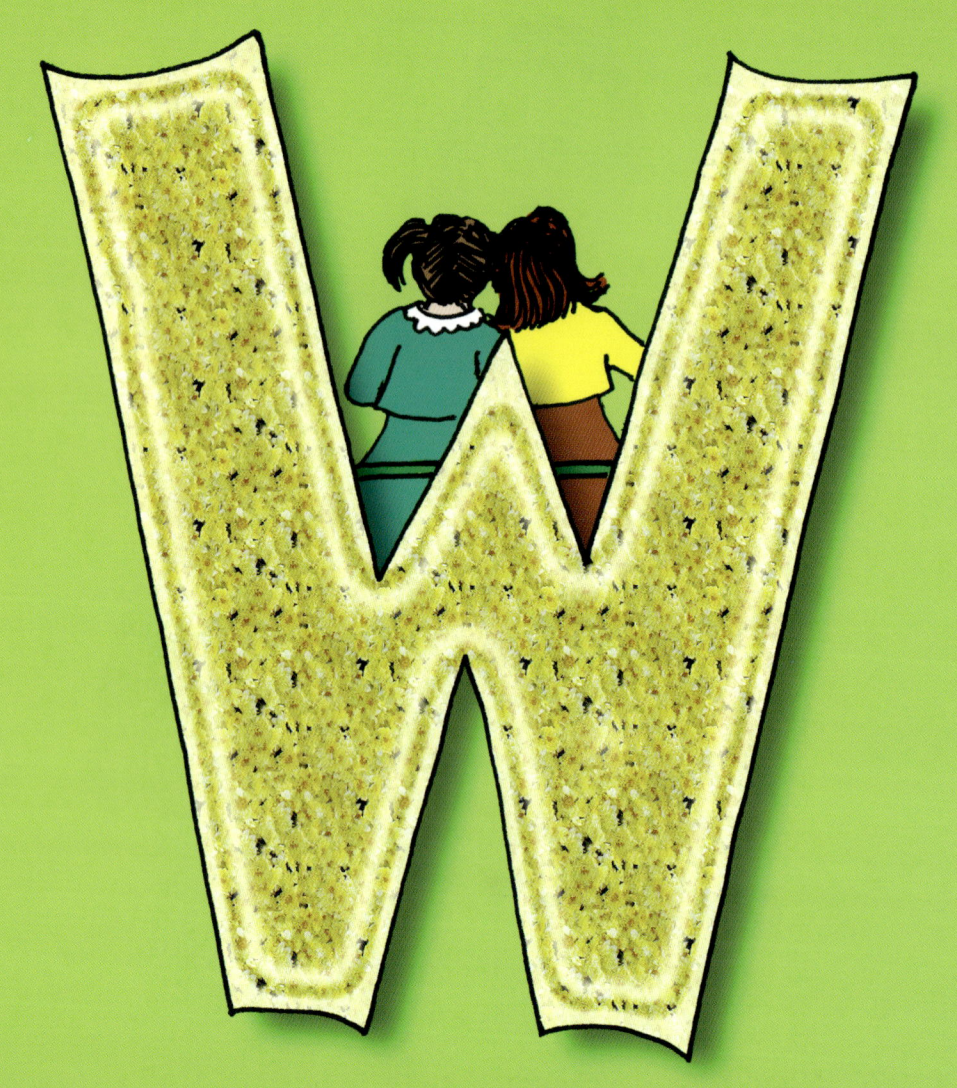

Whispering in front of others makes people feel uncomfortable. Wait until later, in private, if you have something personal to talk about with a friend.

Wear the right clothes for the event you are going to. Dress "up" for fancy times like graduation parties and weddings. Dress sporty for casual times, like picnics, bowling, theme parks, and play-dates.

X-amine your choice of words —
so that no foul language comes to a nice party.

"**X**-cuse me, please"...take all cell phone calls off to the side, away from the table and away from where other people are having a conversation.

Y

You will need to check with the party-giver before bringing along an extra person who was not invited – even if it's a sister or brother or someone staying with you. Being considerate gives the host time to plan for more food and favors.

Yes, you love to be with your pet – so ask your host before you bring it along to a party or into their house.

Zip to a private place or the restroom to comb your hair and do other grooming.

Zoom as soon as you can to return anything you borrowed from a pal: like a book, a jacket, a game, or some athletic equipment.

How it all began...

You've Got Manners Enterprises began with a family road trip – a 1,000 mile vacation through Canada the summer of 2002.

To pass the time among our three generations in a mini-van, the game of naming and playing with table manner ideas became our car activity and then a book.

Soon after the first book on "Table Tips" was published, a series evolved—looking at all types of manners that kids come in contact with, such as social, school time, and how to say things with kindness and truth.

Pictured here is the Five Member Advisory Board for YGM Enterprises, who inspires this venture, with the author Louise Elerding—referred to as "Grandy" by her five sensational grandkids.

Their quarterly Board meetings are generating ideas and decisions for the future, while seeing all possibilities through the eyes of "kids."

At right, the Advisory Board.
From the top of the tree, down and left to right:
Jason, Tyler, Alyssa, Amanda, Louise, Emily

Certificate of Special Achievement

JUST WATCH ME

_____
(Your Name)

I know my Party Pointers from A to Z

and

I'VE GOT SOCIAL MANNERS!

About Louise Elerding

Louise Elerding, AICI, CIP is a Personal Appearance Coach, author, speaker, Image industry trainer, Fashion Feng Shui Facilitator/Trainer, and owner of Professional Image Partners at The Color Studio in Burbank, CA since 1983.

Individuals, businesses, and groups employ Louise to align their inner strengths with their outward appearance - from personal issues to company branding.

Louise is a charter member of the Association of Image Consultants International, AICI, having served as International President 1996-97. She received the esteemed 1999 Award of Excellence from AICI for her contributions to this worldwide industry organization.

In 2001 she was inducted into the International Who's Who of Professional & Business Women's HALL of FAME.

Louise has been quoted in numerous Image books, articles, and publications, among them: Glamour Magazine, L.A. Business Journal, Maximum Style-Rodale Press, the Chicago Tribune, Baltimore Sun, Pacific Sun, One World Live, and CNN.com. Louise also appears on local cable television.

Along with these books, her "Table Manners!" teaching curriculum is being used across the country.

...and we've got Table Manner classes!

Mannersmart — 2 classes: 1 hour each

A basic introduction to Dining Etiquette for ages 11-14.
Experience manners from approaching the table to polite exiting, and the subtle details in between.

Manners 4 Us — 2 classes: 1 hour each

Simple manner-friendly table tips for ages 6-10.
Learn how dining etiquette at the elementary level can be fun.

Teaparty Techniques — 2 classes: 30 minutes each

For boys and girls, ages 3-5 (and their guest bear/doll friends).
Early manner-awareness, with napkin practice, passing techniques, & social introductions.

For more information on classes, teaching manuals, and curriculum licensing
call 1-800-326-8953 or email: MannersA2Z@aol.com

To locate an Etiquette Consultant in your area, call us for a Certified Image Professional
in the Association of Image Consultants International (AICI).

Visit our website: www.youvegotmanners.com

INDEX

Arrive on time	... 7
Before breakfast	... 9
Being nice	...36
Birthday person	...22
Borrowing	...57
Breaking something	...32
Canceling	...12
Cell phones	...53
Computers	...11
Doors held open	...13
Dressing well	...51
Excused from table	...15
Eye contact	...14
Feeling included	...17
Gear storage	...35
Good sportsmanship	...18
Grooming	...56
Handing gifts	...19
Helping yourself	...20
House rules	...21
Interrupting	...44
Jokes	...24
Knocking	...27
Language	...52
Listening	...29
Making beds	...31

Packing up	...37
Party cleanup	...25
Party ending	...48
Party-pouter	...23
Pets	...55
Phone answering	...33
Phone permission	...47
Picking up	...10
Promises	...26
Quiet time	...38
Rearranging furniture	...41
Receiving gifts	...45
RSVP	...40
Say goodbye	...42
Second helpings	...16
Shaking hands	...43
Sharing	...34
Shy	...30
Stand up	...39
Substitute food	...46
Taking turns	...28
Thank-you notes	... 8
Toilet seat cover	...37
TV permission	... 6
Uninvited guests	...54
Visiting elderly	...49
Whispering	...50

You've Got Manners! Series

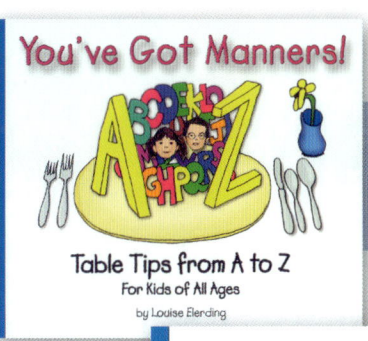

You've Got Manners!
Table Tips from A to Z for Kids of All Ages

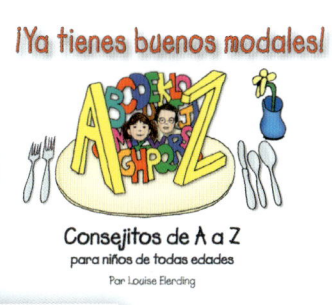

¡Ya tienes buenos modales!
Consejitos de A a Z Para niños de todas edades

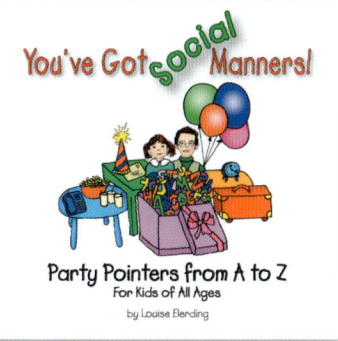

You've Got SOCIAL Manners!
Party Pointers from A to Z for Kids of All Ages

Appearing in 2006:
You've Got RESPECTFUL Manners!
What to Say When You Don't Know How
Tactful Tips from A to Z for Kids of All Ages.

See you around!

Bring your manners with you wherever you go!